CONTENTS

CROWDS OF CRUSTACEANS

Many well-known animals belong to the group of invertebrates known as crustaceans. Crabs, lobsters, shrimp, and barnacles are among the most familiar crustaceans, but the group also includes a large variety of other lesser-known forms. In fact, there are some 45,000 species, or kinds, of crustaceans!

Crabs are some of the most familiar types of crustacean.

WHAT ARE CRUSTACEANS?

THERESE SHEA

Britannica
Educational Publishing

IN ASSOCIATION WITH

ROSEN
EDUCATIONAL SERVICES

Published in 2017 by Britannica Educational Publishing (a trademark of Encyclopædia Britannica, Inc.) in association with The Rosen Publishing Group, Inc.
29 East 21st Street, New York, NY 10010

Distributed exclusively by Rosen Publishing.
To see additional Britannica Educational Publishing titles, go to rosenpublishing.com.

First Edition

Britannica Educational Publishing
J.E. Luebering: Executive Director, Core Editorial
Mary Rose McCudden: Editor, Britannica Student Encyclopedia

Rosen Publishing
Bernadette Davis: Editor
Nelson Sá: Art Director
Brian Garvey: Designer
Cindy Reiman: Photography Manager

Library of Congress Cataloging-in-Publication Data

Names: Shea, Therese, author.
Title: What are crustaceans? / Therese Shea.
Description: First edition. | New York : Britannica Educational Publishing in association with Rosen Educational Services, 2017. | Series: Let's find out! Marine life | Includes bibliographical references and index.
Identifiers: LCCN 2016029705 | ISBN 9781508103851 (library bound) | ISBN 9781508103868 (pbk.)
 | ISBN 9781508103134 (6-pack)
Subjects: LCSH: Crustaceans—Juvenile literature.
Classification: LCC QL437.2 .S54 2016 | DDC 595.3—dc23
LC record available at https://lccn.loc.gov/2016029705

Manufactured in China

Photo credits: Cover, p. 1, interior pages background image mohd farid/Shutterstock.com; pp. 4–5 © Kevin Griffin/Alamy Stock Photo; p. 5 Mr.TJ/Shutterstock.com; p. 6 Robert Taylor/Shutterstock.com; p. 7 Eric V. Grave/Photo Researchers; p. 8 Hans Hillewaert/File:Tanaissus lilljeborgi.jpg/CC BY-SA 4.0; p. 9 Dan Boone/U.S. Fish and Wildlife Service; p. 10 © Merriam-Webster Inc.; pp. 10–11 Enziarro; p. 12 Auscape/Universal Images Group/Getty Images; p. 13 © Sabena Jane Blackbird/Alamy Stock Photo; p. 14 Lebendkulturen.de/Shutterstock.com; p. 15 Mauro Rodrigues/Shutterstock.com; p. 16 Wolfgang Poelzer/WaterFrame/Getty Images; p. 17 E.R. Degginger/Bruce Coleman Inc.; p. 18 Encyclopædia Britannica, Inc.; p. 19 Tony Florio/Science Source/Getty Images; p. 20 © Ericos/Fotolia; p. 21 Cuson/Shutterstock.com; p. 22 Anthony Mercieca/Root Resources/EB Inc.; p. 23 © Colin Marshall/FLPA/Minden Pictures; pp. 24–25 f11photo/Shutterstock.com; p. 25 I. Noyan Yilmaz/Shutterstock.com; p. 26 ullstein bild/Getty Images; p. 27 McClatchy DC/Tribune News Service/Getty Images; p. 28 Eric Hayes/© Comstock; p. 29 NASA Climate Resource Center. Data: National Oceanic and Atmospheric Administration.

Shrimp have thin shells that they shed several times throughout their life.

COMPARE AND CONTRAST

Some animals other than crustaceans have shells, too. What are some similarities between a shrimp's shell and a turtle's shell? What are some differences?

The word "crustacean" comes from the Latin word *crusta*, meaning "shell." All crustaceans have a hard but flexible exoskeleton, or outer shell, and two pairs of antennas, or feelers. Crustaceans are found mainly in water. However, a more specific definition of crustaceans is difficult. This is because there are many differences— in size, features, and habitats—among crustaceans.

CREATURES GREAT AND SMALL

Crustaceans differ greatly in size. The heaviest crustacean is the American lobster. It can reach a weight of 44 pounds (20 kilograms). The longest crustacean is the giant Japanese spider crab. Its legs can stretch up to 12 feet (3.7 meters). The Tasmanian giant crab can weigh as much as 31 pounds

American lobsters like this one are found off the East Coast of North America.

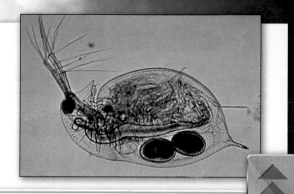

THINK ABOUT IT

Scientists are still discovering new species of crustaceans. What is one reason that you think some species are hard to find?

This water flea is shown as about 15 times larger than its normal size.

(14 kilograms). The average weight of the Alaskan king crab is 10 pounds (4.5 kilograms), but it can grow to over 20 pounds (9 kilograms).

At the other end of the scale, water fleas, fairy shrimp, and brine shrimp are some of the smallest crustaceans. Most are shorter than 0.25 inch (6 millimeters). Water fleas may only grow to be 0.009 inch (0.25 millimeter) long. Although water fleas are almost microscopic in size, they are an important food source for many freshwater fishes.

Habitats Far and Wide

Crustaceans live in oceans, seas, lakes, and rivers throughout the world. They can be found in fresh water, seawater, and inland brines. Some swim in open waters. Other species live at the bottom of the sea. Rocky, sandy, and muddy areas are all homes to crustaceans. Moreover,

VOCABULARY
Brines are naturally occurring sources of water with an unusually high amount of salt.

Tanaids like this one are bottom dwellers. They prefer shallow waters or the deep ocean.

Dungeness crabs are found along the Pacific coast from Alaska to California.

crustaceans can be found from the Arctic to the Antarctic.

The crustaceans called amphipods can live in ocean trenches deeper than 5.5 miles (9 kilometers), while water fleas can live in mountain lakes that are as high as 3 miles (5 km) above sea level.

Some crustaceans are amphibious—that means they are able to live both on land and in water. These include some kinds of crabs and wood lice.

A Breakdown of the Body

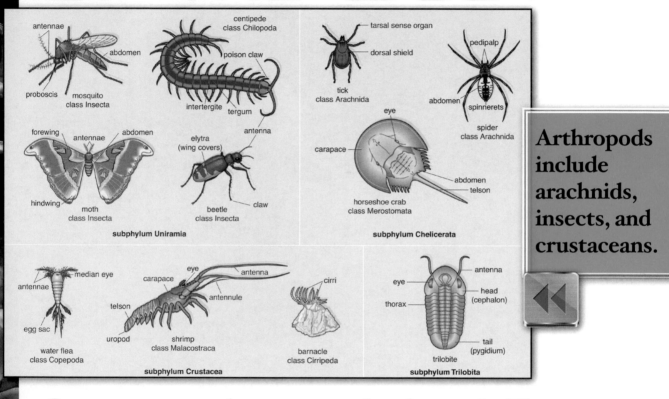

subphylum Uniramia

antennae — abdomen
proboscis — mosquito class Insecta

centipede class Chilopoda
poison claw
intertergite — tergum
antenna

forewing — antennae — abdomen
hindwing — moth class Insecta

elytra (wing covers)
beetle class Insecta
claw

subphylum Chelicerata

tarsal sense organ
dorsal shield
tick class Arachnida

pedipalp
abdomen — spinnerets
spider class Arachnida

eye
carapace
horseshoe crab class Merostomata
abdomen
telson

subphylum Crustacea

median eye
antennae
telson
egg sac
water flea class Copepoda
uropod

carapace — eye — antenna
antennule
shrimp class Malacostraca

cirri
barnacle class Cirripeda

subphylum Trilobita

antenna
eye
thorax
head (cephalon)
trilobite
tail (pygidium)

> Arthropods include arachnids, insects, and crustaceans.

Crustaceans are a huge group of arthropods. The basic crustacean body is usually made up of a number of segments, or sections. The exoskeleton covers each segment to protect the crustacean from harm.

Like lobsters and crabs, crayfish like this one have strong pincers.

At the front end of the body is a region called the acron. This is the head, or forms part of the head, on most crustaceans. At this end, adult crustaceans often have antennas pointing from the top-front area of the head and mandibles, or jaws that extend from their mouths.

Several pairs of limbs grow from the middle section of the body. Many species have different types of limbs for walking, swimming, or mating. Some species have limbs with pincers, or claws.

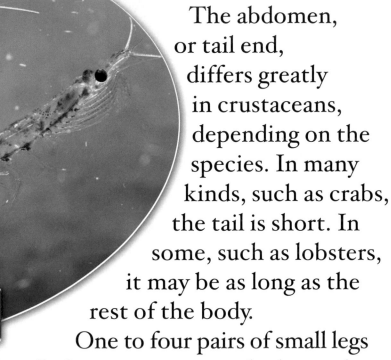

The abdomen, or tail end, differs greatly in crustaceans, depending on the species. In many kinds, such as crabs, the tail is short. In some, such as lobsters, it may be as long as the rest of the body.

One to four pairs of small legs called swimmerets may be located on the underside of a crustacean's abdomen. Swimmerets are used for swimming, breathing, carrying eggs, and other functions.

Krill breathe through gills found in their legs.

THINK ABOUT IT

Crabs that live out of water use gills to breathe, but they must keep the gills moist at all times. How do you think they do this?

An inside view of a crab shows its gills.

Larger species of crustaceans breathe using gills. Even crustaceans that live on land rely on gills to breathe. Smaller crustaceans do not require gills. Gases moving across the surface of their body are enough to keep them alive.

KINDS OF CRUSTACEANS

A major group of small crustaceans are the copepods. These are usually bottom-dwelling forms or zooplankton, which are tiny floating animals. Most crustaceans that are parasites are copepods.

These cyclops are tiny copepods that live in freshwater and salt water habitats.

14

They commonly attach themselves to fish. Some copepods are an essential food source for marine (seawater) organisms, including many different kinds of whales.

The pill bug rolls into a ball to protect itself from harm.

Ostracods, or seed shrimp, are tiny marine or freshwater crustaceans. Their flattened shells give them the appearance of clams. Most live near the sea bottom. They are omnivores, which means they eat both plants and animals. They are also scavengers, consuming dead organisms and waste.

The group of crustaceans called isopods has mostly marine forms, but the group includes the land-living sow bugs and pill bugs, or wood lice. Isopods are flat and usually gray.

A crustacean group that is related to the isopods is the amphipods. This group is also mostly marine, and they look similar to small shrimp. Amphipods that live on sand beaches are also called sand hoppers or sand fleas. Amphipods are important food for many

THINK ABOUT IT

It is illegal to catch some crustaceans, such as the Alaskan king crab, during certain times of the year. What might happen if such laws were not in place?

Freshwater crayfish like this one can look a lot like lobsters.

animals, including fishes, penguins, and seals.

Barnacles are mostly marine crustaceans. Adult barnacles remain in one spot throughout their lives. They attach to any solid surface including rocks, the underside of ships, and even turtles. Some species of barnacles are parasites in crabs and other crustaceans. Barnacles are filter feeders, straining plankton from the water that swirls around them.

The most important crustaceans to humans are the decapods. Many of these crustaceans are valuable sources of food. Lobsters, crabs, shrimp, and crayfish are all decapods. Decapods are usually omnivores.

This amphipod is called a hopper because of the movement it makes.

ROOM TO GROW

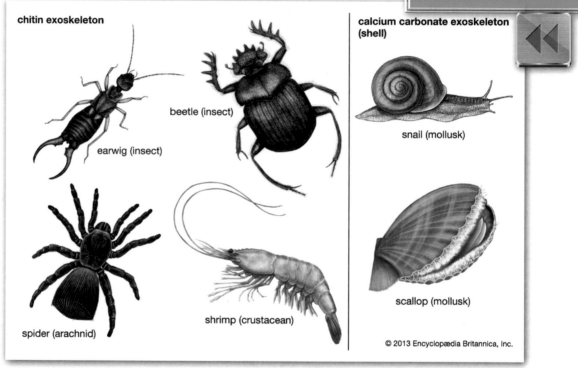

chitin exoskeleton

earwig (insect)

beetle (insect)

spider (arachnid)

shrimp (crustacean)

calcium carbonate exoskeleton (shell)

snail (mollusk)

scallop (mollusk)

© 2013 Encyclopædia Britannica, Inc.

The crustacean's exoskeleton is made of a hard protein substance called chitin. It protects the body and provides a place for muscles to attach. The thickness of the exoskeleton can vary from very thin, as in some

THINK ABOUT IT

Crabs that have lost legs can grow them back slowly through a series of molts. However, older crabs may never grow the missing leg back to a normal size. Why do you think this is?

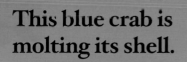

This blue crab is molting its shell.

copepods, to a rigid shell, as in crabs.

Crustaceans molt, or shed, their exoskeletons several times as they grow. First, the old exoskeleton separates from the body. Then, new cells are created to form the new exoskeleton. The old exoskeleton splits and is shed wholly or in parts.

Different species molt a different number of times from when they are born to adulthood. Molting may continue throughout the life of the adult, but it does not occur as often.

PROTECTION FROM PREDATORS

Though many crustaceans are predators, they all face danger from other kinds of predators. Some crustaceans are eaten by fish and octopuses. Free-floating zooplankton are consumed by fish and larger marine animals, including whales. Birds eat crabs and other crustaceans.

Crustaceans have developed several adaptations for predatory protection. Some have colors or patterns

Blue whales like this one depend on krill as a food source.

COMPARE AND CONTRAST

Male fiddler crabs and ghost crabs grow one claw much larger than the other. How do you think this makes life different for them than other kinds of crustaceans?

that help them blend in with their environment. Others burrow into the ground to avoid detection. Pill bugs are land-dwelling crustaceans that roll themselves into tiny balls for protection.

Some decapods such as lobsters and crabs use their front pinching claws to defend themselves and to acquire food.

Male fiddler crabs hold their large claw like a musician holds a fiddle.

FRESH CRUSTACEANS

Crustacean reproduction and development from egg to adult are highly complex. The males usually have certain appendages used in the reproductive process. The females of most species carry their eggs on their bodies in some manner. Some female crustaceans, however, release their eggs into the water.

Some crustaceans hatch into a larva called a nauplius that does not look like the adult. Its body has only one

A barnacle starts as a naupilus. After it attaches to a solid object, it develops into an adult.

This harlequin crab is laying eggs.

segment and three sets of appendages. The nauplius body changes with each molt.

Other crustacean young emerge from eggs looking like adults. This is true for most isopods and amphipods and for some decapods, including freshwater crabs and crayfish.

COMPARE AND CONTRAST

Most barnacles have both male and female reproductive organs. Why do you think this is helpful for barnacles, compared to other crustaceans?

CRUCIAL CRUSTACEANS

Crustaceans of all sizes play a key role in their food chains. They help keep ocean life balanced by eating plants and animals (alive or dead) or by being the food of larger animals. Without crustaceans, the delicate balance of the food chain would be disrupted.

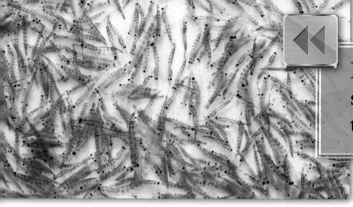

Krill are an important food source for many animals in the sea.

Crustaceans have proved to be very useful to humans. For instance, scientists have learned a lot about genetics from studying the genes of water fleas. Shrimp shells can be used to make an environmentally friendly plastic. Barnacles are crushed and used as fertilizer. Brine shrimp and water fleas are used as fish food in aquariums, and hermit crabs are popular pets. Crustaceans are also an important source of food for humans. Crabs, lobsters, and shrimp can be found in restaurants and markets all over the world.

THINK ABOUT IT

Why are the decapods especially important crustaceans to humans?

These Japanese spider crabs clean the bottom of the ocean by eating dead animals. They also feed on mollusks and plants.

PESTS AND PARASITES

Crustaceans can cause problems, too. Parasitic crustaceans get their food from their host and often harm them. The parasites are also known to pass deadly illnesses on to their host.

The amphipods nicknamed "killer shrimp" have become an invasive species in many lakes and rivers in Europe. The killer shrimp kill water creatures and

Wood lice sometimes eat young plants but rarely cause significant damage.

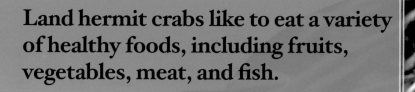

Land hermit crabs like to eat a variety of healthy foods, including fruits, vegetables, meat, and fish.

then often do not even eat them.

Crustaceans can mean trouble for farms. Burrowing crabs drain water from rice paddies, exposing the roots of the plants to the sun. Land crabs and crayfish can harm tomato and cotton crops.

Large groups of barnacles cause damage to the bodies of ships and can reduce the speed of the ships through water. The shipping industry makes great efforts to control barnacles.

VOCABULARY

An **invasive species** is a living thing that spreads into a new area and threatens the balance of the ecosystem there.

CARING ABOUT CRUSTACEANS

Crustaceans are essential animals in food chains, including as food for people. The health of crustaceans is therefore important for their habitats, as well as for humankind. However, human activities are threatening crustacean populations. One problem is overfishing. Countries have put rules in place to make sure that people do not catch so many crustaceans that the animals would disappear.

Overfishing is not the only threat to crustacean populations. When people burn fossil

Lobsters are caught with cages baited with dead fish. These cages are called lobster pots.

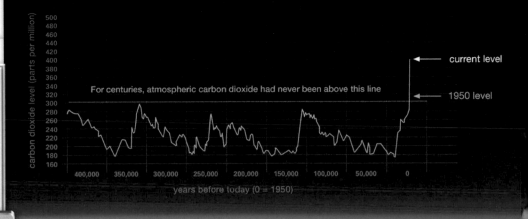

Levels of carbon dioxide have increased in recent years.

carbon dioxide level (parts per million)

For centuries, atmospheric carbon dioxide had never been above this line

current level

1950 level

years before today (0 = 1950)

fuels for energy, a gas called carbon dioxide is released into Earth's atmosphere. The carbon dioxide also gets into the waters of the oceans. This has raised the ocean's acidity. Scientists have discovered that the increased acidity makes it harder for crustaceans to form their exoskeletons, which are necessary for their survival.

Without changes in human behavior in years to come, the future of the incredible animal called the crustacean is uncertain.

THINK ABOUT IT

Fossil fuels, including oil, coal, and natural gas, are a source of energy for people. What other sources of energy can people use that might not hurt the environment?

GLOSSARY

adaptation A change in an organism or its parts that fits it better for the conditions of its environment.

appendage A body part (such as an arm or a leg) connected to the main part of the body.

arachnid An eight-legged creature with a two-part body.

burrow A hole in the ground made by an animal for shelter or protection. Also, to make a hole in the ground in which to live or hide.

ecosystem A community of living things interacting with their environment.

fertilizer A substance such as manure or a chemical used to make soil produce larger or more plant life.

flexible Capable of being bent.

fossil fuel A fuel (such as coal, oil, or natural gas) that is formed in the earth from plant or animal remains.

genetics The study of how features pass from parents to their young.

gills Filters on the side of an animal's body that are used for breathing.

habitat The place or type of place where a plant or animal naturally or normally lives or grows.

insect A small, six-legged animal with a three-part body.

invertebrate A creature that has no backbone.

mollusk Any of a large group of invertebrate animals (such as snails, clams, and octopuses) with a soft body lacking segments and usually enclosed in a shell containing calcium.

predator An animal that lives by killing and eating other animals.

protein Any of numerous substances that consist of many compounds essential for life and that are supplied by various foods.

reproduction The process by which plants and animals produce offspring.

trench A long narrow steep-sided depression in the ocean floor.

FOR MORE INFORMATION

Books

Bodden, Valerie. *Crabs*. Mankato, MN: Creative Education, 2017.

Moore, Heidi. *Giant Isopods and Other Crafty Crustaceans*. Chicago, IL: Raintree, 2012.

Pallotta, Jerry. *Lobster vs. Crab*. New York, NY: Scholastic, 2014.

Parker, Rick. *Aquaculture Science*. New York, NY: Cengage Learning, 2012.

Roesser, Marie. *Mantis Shrimp*. New York, NY: Gareth Stevens Publishing, 2015.

Websites

Because of the changing nature of internet links, Rosen Publishing has developed an online list of websites related to the subject of this book. This site is updated regularly. Please use this link to access this list:

http://www.rosenlinks.com/LFO/crust

Index